Classic Marques

JAGUAR

Classic Marques

JAGUAR

Paul Skilleter

K222 JAG

Grange BOOKS

Published by Grange Books
An Imprint of Grange Books Limited
The Grange
Grange Yard
London
SE1 3AG

Published 1993

ISBN 1-85627-248-6

Produced by
Bison Books Ltd
Kimbolton House
117A Fulham Road
London SW3 6RL

Printed in Hong Kong

PAGE 1: An XK 120 fixed-head coupe prepared for historic rallying.

PAGES 2-3: Jaguar's latest supercar, the XJ220, in a village in Warwickshire, England.

THESE PAGES: A V12 E-type open seater.

Contents

CHAPTER 1
Coachbuilder to Car Maker

The story of Jaguar contains many surprises; the first being that the car itself was never planned as part of a great strategy, but emerged by chance from a chain of events which started in 1921 in someone's back yard. Even then, that someone was not Jaguar founder-to-be William Lyons himself, but one William Walmsley, who was building side-cars for motorcycles in the double garage behind his parents' house in Blackpool, Lancashire.

Walmsley had moved from Stockport in Cheshire to Britain's most popular seaside resort in 1921; and King Edward Avenue was soon graced by examples of his spectacular, polished aluminum, octagonal-shaped sidecar. Now also living in this staid, middle-class road was a 20-year-old motorcycle enthusiast rapidly becoming bored with his car salesman's job. William Lyons saw how young men like himself were attracted to the 'Swallow' sidecar's dashing looks, and having struck up an acquaintanceship with Walmsley, eventually persuaded him to go into business with him producing the chair in quantity.

Both sets of parents were keen to help, Walmsley senior because Walmsley Junior was already 30 and lacking a proper career, and Lyons senior because it was clear that young William didn't want to enter the family piano and music business. Accordingly they jointly guaranteed an overdraft facility of £1000 and the Swallow Sidecar Company was in business – officially constituted on 11 September 1922, a few days after Bill Lyons' 21st birthday on September 4th.

There followed a spectacular period of growth for just as Lyons had hoped, the Swallow sidecar had a national (and indeed international) appeal. The model range expanded; a move was made to a much larger factory; and the Model 4 chair was soon being made at the rate of over 50 a week. 'One-off' coachbuilding jobs were now being taken on, and importantly, in 1927 the first series-production coachbuilt body was made on an Austin 7 chassis – Sir Herbert Austin's brilliantly successful baby car.

The Austin Seven Swallow's pretty, rounded-tail lines set a pattern for the next five years, and an unexpectedly large order from the big motor distributor Henlys in London for 500 Swallow Sevens elevated the business into a level far higher than that enjoyed by most other contemporary British coachbuilders. It also forced a move from Blackpool to Coventry in the heart of industrial England, where skilled labor was more available, and in 1928 an old shell-filling factory at Holbrooks was leased and renovated.

Still funded largely by the sales success of the Model 4 sidecar, the range of coachbuilt car bodies was rapidly extended to other makes besides Austin – including Wolseley, Fiat, Swift and Standard. Despite the gloomy economic

LEFT: Harley-Davidson and Brough Superior motorcycles – the actual machines ridden by Lyons and Walmsley in the 1920s – with a very early Austin Seven Swallow outside the Cocker Street factory where it was built.

RIGHT: The 1929 Austin Swallow sedan.

BELOW LEFT: Lyons' first car was the strikingly styled S.S.1 two-plus-two coupe of 1931. Later variants included the 'fast-back' Airline of 1935 (ABOVE LEFT).

RIGHT: Colorful paint schemes were a Swallow hall-mark, as displayed by this Austin Seven open two seater.

climate, Swallow grew quickly as the merits of its products – style, bright duo-tone color schemes not previously seen outside the US, and highly competitive pricing – fueled sales in what was really the 'custom' end of the car market.

Lyons' eye for a distinctive and harmonious shape was already very evident, but equally important was his grasp of economics. Swallow could make bodies quicker and more cheaply than any other similar company thanks to highly accurate jig-built frames requiring virtually no hand-fitting in assembly – plus tight organization throughout the plant and close monitoring of costs. Some 2500 Austin Swallow Sevens were built (an amazingly high number), as were 530 Wolseley-based semi-sportscars.

It was again largely on Henlys' prompting that Lyons made his bid to launch a marque name of his own, and the S.S.1 which appeared at the October 1931 British Motor Show made a great impression. This low, mean-looking coupe used a chassis and drive train made and assembled by the Standard Motor Company a few miles away at Canley; an arrangement which relieved Swallow of having to fund the purchase of manufacturing plant. That helped explain the new car's spectacularly low price of £310, which was little more than the cost then of an ordinary, medium-sized family sedan.

In fact the flat-head 2054cc or 2552cc straight-six engines used didn't exactly provide the S.S.1 with the speed its looks suggested, nor was the original body – with a roof-line hastily raised on the eve of the show – the most balanced Lyons design ever. However, over 500 of the

70mph, 'helmet wing' coupe were made, and the revised model of September 1932 was a vastly better machine. Horsepower was upped from 55 to 62bhp for the larger engined model, and the wheelbase was extended by 7in to 9ft 11in, which, together with a new body with a continuous wingline flowing from front to rear, made it a handsome and quite sporting coupe capable of over 80mph.

An open tourer joined the range in March 1933 and in 1934 the smaller S.S.2 model, another 1931 debutante, was substantially improved and was offered with open bodywork too. Also in 1934 the S.S.1 Airline variant arrived, a pillarless two-door sedan with a curved 'fast back' reflecting a contemporary craze. This car is notable for being one of the few models to be openly criticized by Lyons for its technical imperfections, but it at least served to dissuade him from ever again blindly following fashion. Yet even then, 624 Airlines were made, a very high figure that would have been the envy of many other British coachbuilders for their mainstream model.

But what did the initials 'S.S.' stand for? There were undoubtedly several sources of inspiration for the choice, beginning with Lyons' keen appreciation of George Brough's rapid motorcycles of superb quality which had the model designations of S.S.80, S.S.90 etc. and which both Lyons and Walmsley rode. Then, due to the link with Standard, the letters could be taken to indicate Standard Swallow or Swallow Sports (to please Standard's chief John Black). But William Lyons was quite clear about it. The meaning, he said, was never resolved . . .

CHAPTER 2

S.S. Breeds a Jaguar

By the end of 1934 William Lyons had largely succeeded in establishing SS as an individual marque and in October of that year he and Walmsley floated a new limited company more appropriate to it – SS Cars Ltd. However, at the company's first AGM in November, Walmsley proffered his resignation. The older man had never possessed Lyons' ambition, and the two partners had become increasingly irritated with each other – Lyons because he felt Walmsley to be uncommitted and a drag on progress, and Walmsley because he preferred a gentler pace of life to the pursuit of ever-bigger goals. He sold out and departed a rich man (he died in 1961; Sir William sent a deputy to his funeral).

Lyons was now where he wanted to be – in total charge. For the next 38 years he would be, in effect, a dictator, taking every major decision himself; true, he would sometimes discuss policy with his fellow directors, but his would be the final judgment and board meetings were mere formalities. And who is to say that in overall terms this was anything but an immensely successful arrangement?

Meanwhile the succession of new models continued. In the spring of 1935 came the most exotic S.S.1 variant, the drophead coupe (with its fully-lined top that disappeared into the rear trunk) and Lyons' first true sportscar, the S.S.90 (constructed on a shortened version of the S.S.1 chassis). This superbly styled two-seater with its imposing radiator, large headlamps and multi-louvered hood was powered by a slightly modified version of the 2663cc Standard six cylinder S.S.1 engine. This gave the car a smooth, quick off the mark performance but lacked the muscle to produce real punch. Lyons knew that if credibility was to be established for SS in the true performance-car catagory, help was badly needed.

This was supplied by two key men early in 1935. Firstly, Brooklands motor cycle tuning wizard Harry Weslake was retained to design a new overhead valve cylinder head for the Standard engine. Then on the advice of Standard's engineering department (on which Lyons had hitherto depended, SS having no proper engineering section), a former Standard engineer who had transferred to Humber was hired as SS Cars' first chief engineer.

William Heynes recounted in later years how, during the several interviews that had transpired, Lyons proclaimed his intention to one day produce the best luxury motor car in the world. The task of turning the enterprising though still

LEFT: The S.S.90 was Bill Lyons' first true sportscar and evolved into the SS Jaguar 100.

RIGHT: The S.S.90 radiator grille carried the type name on the lamp bar.

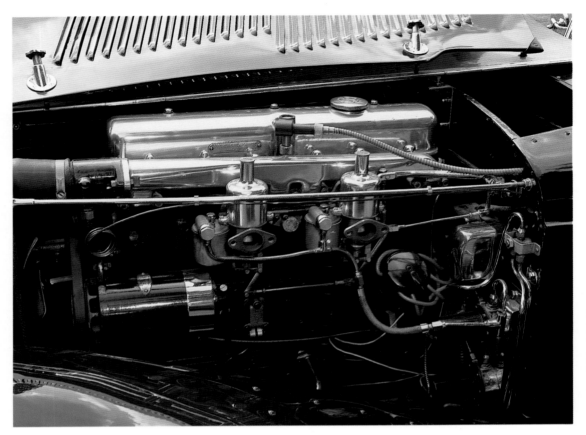

LEFT: The 2½-liter engine, seen here in an SS 100, with its new DHV cylinder head, provided the new Jaguar range with true performance.

RIGHT AND BELOW RIGHT: One of 190 2½-liter SS 100s; this 1936 car (18034) was owned by the author.

slightly odd SS into a world-class car was a daunting one, but Heynes approached the job with calm deliberation and common-sense, despite the requirement to produce a new range of cars in time for the September 1935 Motor Show.

There was no time or money to use anything except the existing S.S.1 frame, but Heynes applied sound improvements to it. He replaced the inconsistent Bendix cable brakes with the highly efficient Girling rod type, added bigger steering joints, and successfully installed the new Weslake-head engine – which to everyone's joy was found to produce 100bhp, or some 30bhp more than before.

The new cars which were announced in September enjoyed a new name too – 'Jaguar'; selected by Lyons himself. Star of the Motor Show was the SS Jaguar 2½-liter sedan, a superbly handsome, full four-seater with styling obviously inspired by all that was best in traditional British coachbuilding. To many the car seemed like a down-sized Bentley – but at an even more down-sized price, for at £395 the new Jaguar appeared impossibly cheap, even to Lyons' own dealer organization. The Press in turn soon discovered that this time beauty was more than skin-deep. *The Autocar* magazine recorded a 'two-way' maximum speed of 85.7mph, which among the 82 cars the magazine had tested, was 'exceeded only by others having considerably larger engine capacities, and costing from twice to nearly four times the price.'

There was a baby sister too. This was the '1½-liter', though the smallest Jaguar ever made actually had an engine size of 1608cc. Side-valved, it wasn't very fast – 70mph at best – but at £285 it was extraordinarily good value, and cheaper than comparable 1½-liter sedans from established British companies like Riley. This model was highly tactical: it was sold virtually at cost, to boost sales

volumes far above those achieved by conventional specialist car-makers like Daimler, Rolls-Royce and Lagonda. The result of this was to reduce unit costs on parts shared by the larger car – on which a good profit was made.

Two other Jaguars emerged in 1935: the Tourer was an updated version of the four-seat open S.S.1, with the 2½-liter ohv engine and chassis improvements, while the SS 100 was an up-grade of the S.S.90, again with the Weslake-head 2½-liter engine and Girling brakes.

Overshadowed by the new sedans at the time, and built in relatively small quantities, the SS Jaguar 100 was to become one of Britain's outstanding sportscars of the 1930s. Thanks to the new engine and a relatively light weight, it provided true, 90mph performance; it was also reliable, handled well (though it preferred smooth surfaces!), and above all looked a million dollars. The SS 100 wasn't innovative, but it was an enticing package half the price of anything with a similar performance.

The new Jaguar range was almost embarrassingly successful. In two years, 2,249 1½-liter and 3,444 2½-liter sedans were made, an astonishing total for what was still really a labor-intensive coachbuilding operation. However, even streamlined production couldn't keep up with sales and Lyons took the decision to dispense with the time-consuming wooden body framing and replace it with an all-steel body with outer panels supported by a steel internal structure.

At the same time, William Heynes took the opportunity to design a new chassis with a much stiffer, box-section frame. Three engine sizes were offered. The shorter-wheelbase '1½-liter' shared the same cabin and was powered by a new 1,776cc overhead valve power unit, and the established 2½-liter engine was joined by a new 3,485cc six

cylinder unit, again Standard built, producing 125bhp and giving the 3½-liter sedan a 90mph top speed. For the first time, a drophead style was optional for all three engine sizes.

The change to all-steel bodies was very nearly a disaster. SS contracted with three different suppliers for body panels, but at least one failed to adhere to the patterns they'd been given, and the parts wouldn't fit. Production of the new range was delayed for some months while the problem was sorted out. This very nearly put the company into bankruptcy, but at last, in the early part of 1938, the new Jaguars began to emerge from the Swallow Road factory and, bigger, faster and more luxurious, they proved even more popular.

The SS Jaguar 100 was also offered with the 3½-liter engine, immediately making it one of the fastest production cars in the world. Admittedly an Alfa Romeo 2500 might be quicker, but you'd have to pay £1000 more at least than the £445 asked for the 3½-liter 100. A genuine 100mph was now obtainable, with 60 mph reached in under 11 seconds. This meant considerable success in road rallies, and the 100 became a regular winner of important UK events such as the RAC and Welsh Rallies. It could also give a good account of itself on the famous banked track at Brooklands, a factory-modified 3½-liter running on dope achieving a 118mph lap.

Then came World War II. A few cars were produced in 1940, but soon the entire SS factory was turned over to war work. A great variety of tasks were undertaken, such as the

repair and manufacture of aircraft frames – including Spitfire parts and Meteor jet fuselages. This provided the company with new skills which were to come in very useful after the war had ended.

Postwar saw a change of name. SS, with its Nazi connotations, was unusable and so Jaguar Cars Ltd was born. Not without difficulty – many jigs and tools had been lost or damaged during the war – the prewar range (minus the 100) was put back into production from September 1945, with minor updates and modifications. Importantly, left-hand drive was offered for the first time – the company had always exported its products to a degree, but now it was

essential. Indeed, it was a government requirement as the country fought to pay off the enormous debts it had accumulated in the fight against Hitler.

Some Jaguars found their way to the US, probably selling on antique grandeur as much as anything – they looked very old-fashioned compared to the curvaceous shapes which had been coming from Detroit for some years. Nor was the dealer and parts back-up more than elementary, but all that was to change. Ever since the early 1940s, when it had been realized that the war would be won, the design of a brand new engine had begun – an engine which would help take Jaguar to new heights.

THESE PAGES: Prewar (LEFT) and postwar (RIGHT) 1½-liter Jaguars were sold virtually without profit, but they amortized costs for their rapid 3½-liter 'big sister' (ABOVE).

CHAPTER 3
The XK Arrives

While the 3½-liter Jaguar sedans were about the most rapid four-five seaters you could buy on the British market, William Lyons had known even prewar that they were old-fashioned, and that the engine could not be developed to give much more power reliably. Independent front suspension systems were already under development and during the long war years much time was spent by Lyons, Heynes, ex-Bentley development engineer Walter Hassan, and engine draughtsman Claude Baily, discussing power units. For Lyons required an engine capable of propelling his next big Jaguar sedan at a true 100mph.

It was a brave step by Lyons to place his trust in Heynes' desire to make a quantum leap and go for the then exotic twin overhead camshaft layout for the new power plant. This stemmed from Heynes' enthusiasm for racing motorcycles and motor racing. Before the war, all the best machines had overhead cam engines, but could 'racing' valve gear be made suitable for a luxury sedan, which must be quiet and reliable as well as fast?

To the eternal credit of Heynes and his team, the XK engine which emerged in 1948 fulfilled every one of these qualifications brilliantly. It produced ample power and torque, was sewing-machine smooth, and could run for well over 100,000 miles without major attention. If it had been otherwise it might have sunk the Jaguar marque for good – there was little spare cash for expensive warranty claims or second attempts. As it was, the XK engine was to become Jaguar's backbone and mainstay for 38 years.

Meanwhile, a massively strong new frame had been designed to carry Jaguar's first independent front suspension – essential for good ride qualities. This chassis was in fact

LEFT: The first 240 XK 120s had aluminum bodies.

RIGHT: The cockpit of this early XK120 shows unexpected luxury for a sports machine.

ABOVE RIGHT: The Mk V (1948-1951) was an interim model for Jaguar.

ready well ahead of the body for the intended 100mph sedan, so as an interim measure it was released with an updated version of the prewar style body. The resulting car, termed the Mk V (it was supposed to have been the fifth of five prototypes), came with either the 2½ or 3½-liter push-rod engines. It was announced on 1 October 1948.

It was as an afterthought that Lyons decided to produce a new sportscar for the 1948 Motor Show, intending to gain some publicity. He quickly evolved a two-seater body and put it on a shortened version of the new chassis fitted with the 3442cc XK engine. In anticipation of its top speed, the car was named 'XK 120', and it cost just £1273.

The reception accorded this beautiful machine quite shocked Jaguar. Charles Hornburg, visiting from the US, wanted to buy the first year's entire production. Immediately, plans to build the XK 120 in low-volume with aluminum bodywork were abandoned, and although 240 were indeed so built, tooling for a 'production' steel body was rapidly commissioned to meet the demand. Even then, America could hardly get enough XK 120s.

It was not until October 1950 that Lyons' major preoccupation, his 100mph luxury sedan, could be revealed. The Mk Vll (Bentley had appeared with their Mk Vl in the meantime so Jaguar skipped that designation) used the longer wheelbase version of the same chassis clothed with a handsome, if bulky, all steel body and powered of course by the XK engine. It too was a great sales success, for apart from looking good it was fast, extremely refined, and handled extraordinarily well for its size.

THESE PAGES: Wire wheels became an option for the XK 120 in 1951, when the beautiful fixed-head version was announced.

ABOVE: The XK-powered MK VII sedan was Jaguar's first 100mph sedan.

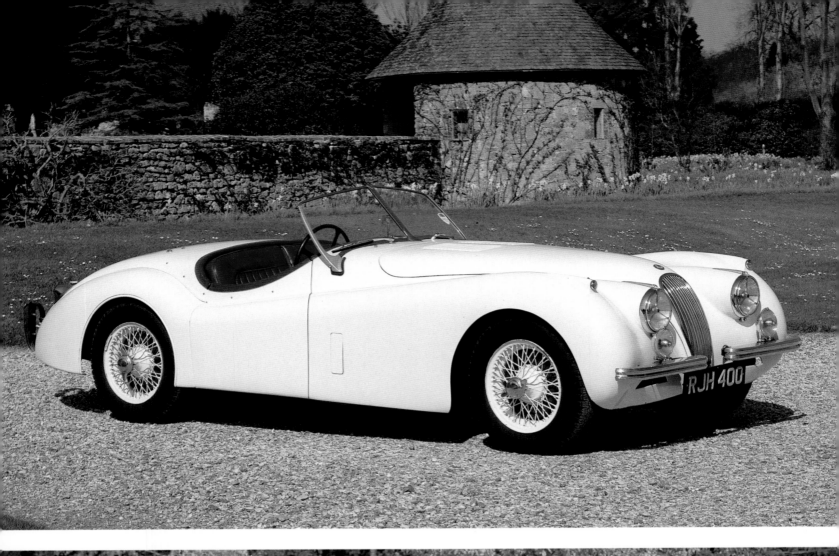

THESE PAGES: The XK 120 roadster (TOP LEFT) was a successful rally car in its day. The drop-head (BELOW LEFT) joined the XK range in April 1953 and was given a veneered dash (RIGHT). Styling nuances of the XK 120 fixed-head are as valid today as they were in 1951 (BELOW).

Jaguar's success in winning the 1951 Le Mans race (see Chapter Five) was enormously important, as it finally banished any remaining criticism that their cars looked rather better than they actually went. Fueled too by the XK 120's prowess in international rallies, world sales greatly increased as a result, and Jaguar became a full member of the motoring establishment.

Over the next four years the existing range was improved and expanded. In March 1951 a delightfully proportioned fixed-head coupe joined the XK 120 roadster, while 'Special Equipment' (including wire wheels and more power) became optional. The XK range was completed in April 1953 by a drop-head coupe, which had wind-up windows and a fully lined top.

Nor was the Mk Vll neglected. It evolved into the Mk VllM in October 1954, with more power and minor exterior and interior updates, while the choice of automatic transmission widened its market even further.

Jaguar soon became Britain's biggest dollar earner. The cars were just right for America – beautiful to look at, pleasant and easy to drive, reliable in their essentials, affordable and fast. Nor, in a country used to 19-foot monsters, were they regarded as anything except neatly sized. The XK 120 certainly repositioned the sportscar. Thanks to its sedan origins, its tremendous performance came with flexibility, quietness and comfort, attributes not formerly associated with rapid two-seaters. Hence its popularity with ladies, and among the fashionable Hollywood set. You didn't have to be a masochist – or an expert – to drive a Jaguar.

This blend of style, performance and value for money was meanwhile having a devastating effect on Britain's specialist car market. In an interesting parallel to what, in a slightly different way, the Japanese did during their onslaught on the luxury car market in the early 1990s, Jaguar in the 1930s and 1950s produced better, faster, cheaper and more exciting looking cars than the opposition could. The result was that many famous firms found they couldn't compete, and either went out of business or became badge-engineered mass-produced vehicles. In the lucrative US market, with Mercedes extremely expensive, there wasn't really any oppposition for Jaguar at all. And yet the best was yet to come.

CHAPTER 4
Jaguar Goes for Volume

Much influenced by the reaction of the American market to the XK 120, the XK 140 of October 1954 brought more room, more protection against parking damage, and even more performance. The engine had been moved forward to provide a larger cockpit, which on the fixed-head and drop-head models allowed two occasional seats to be installed in the back. At a pinch, the XK 140 could now manage a couple of kids or an adult sitting cross-ways.

The open two-seater, though, remained just that and also kept its canvas-and-sticks top augmented by side screens. Nor did it acquire the wood veneer of the other two variants. It was the most favored of XK 140s, and more were made than any other type, the majority of these going to the United States – mostly California.

Rack and pinion steering gave the XK 140 more steering precision, while alterations to the chassis cross-members allowed overdrive to become an option. Operated at the flick of a dashboard switch, the Laycock de Normanville device gave a wonderfully relaxed, 3.19:1, cruising ratio. The optional Special Equipment pack brought wire wheels and spot lamps, while for more performance, the C-type head (which had been available on late XK 120s) could be ordered too, when the engine was rated at 210bhp.

The XK 140 was a straightforward development of an existing theme. Totally new was the 2.4-liter 'compact' sedan announced in September 1955, highly significant because it was Jaguar's first volume car. The fully-tooled body was of unitary construction and much attention had been paid to refinement now that there was no separate chassis frame to insulate the shell from road noise and vibration.

Much of this work was carried out under Heynes' guidance by Robert J. Knight. He used a front sub-frame, mounted on the body via rubber bushes, to carry the new coil-spring suspension, while the cantilevered rear leaf springs were flexibly mounted within steel boxes. The axle was located by both radius arms and a Panhard rod. Power was provided by a new, short-stroke version of the XK engine, still six cylinder for smoothness but with only 2483cc. So with its modern bodyshell – a unique 'teardrop' shape styled by Lyons – great refinement, and all the usual Jaguar leather and veneer inside, the 2.4 sedan was a most sophisticated automobile in which can be seen the origins of the refinement seen in all modern Jaguars.

Although it was a struggle to keep the cost down, the 2.4 at $3700 was priced usefully below the Mk VIIM, providing a

LEFT AND RIGHT: The XK 140 fixed-head had a larger cockpit, a greater glass area, and two-plus-two seating.

lower entry-level to Jaguar motoring. The biggest criticism from the US concerned power, and it wasn't long before this was remedied by the option of the full Special Equipment 210bhp 3.4-liter engine.

This turned the small Jaguar into a virtually unrivaled road burner. It supplanted the Bentley Continental as the world's fastest four-seater production car, was quicker than any stock US automobile, and probably matched most of the hotted-up ones. In 1957, when the 3.4 was released, a 0-60 mph time of 10.4 seconds, a maximum speed of 120mph, and a standing quarter mile of 17.6 seconds, were dynamite for a luxury, four-seat sedan!

Initially the 3.4 was rather too fast for its brakes, as indeed the XK 120 had been. However, the disk brakes that Jaguar had pioneered at Le Mans soon became available, and most 3.4 sedans left the factory with them. That way, the extraordinary performance could be used to the full. Wire wheels became an option on both 2.4 and 3.4 cars, and with the introduction of the 3.4 had come a narrow-slatted, XK 120-style radiator grille, replacing the cast XK 140-type of the original 2.4.

The motor racing fraternity in Europe was not slow to realize the sporting potential of the 3.4. In England, where 'saloon racing' was becoming ever more popular, the 3.4

took over the Mk VII's mantle as the quickest sedan – especially when driven by Jaguar works driver Mike Hawthorn – while on the rallying front, first the 2.4 and then the 3.4 became increasingly competitive. Twins Don and Erle Morley, later to gain even greater fame driving the Austin-Healey 3000 for the BMC works team, won the punishing Tulip Rally in 1959 with their privately-entered 3.4.

In the US, Briggs Cunningham's lead driver Walt Hansgen won a 'compact' race which accompanied the 1959 US Grand Prix at Sebring, while in Australia, David McKay and his gray 3.4 was the man to beat.

Jaguar's big sedan came in for revision during 1956, the Mk VIIM turning into the Mk VIII. A one-piece windscreen replaced the earlier car's divided one, a chrome strip now ran down the sides, the interior was face-lifted and the 210bhp engine became standard.

The years to 1957 had been important. There was now an ideal model range: the affordable 2.4-liter, a range of well-developed sportscars, and a big luxury sedan (the Mk VIII). Most important of all, the 2.4 and 3.4 had brought volume: sales jumped from 5805 cars in 1951, to 17,552 in 1958, thanks chiefly to the 'compacts'. Profits had almost doubled too.

CHAPTER 5
Cat on The Track

Bill Lyons had always been keen on competitions and in his 'teens' had taken part in amateur motorcycling events – perhaps with his 'Daytona' model Harley-Davidson (his favourite bike). After Swallow was in business, he arranged for special 'chairs' to be made for sidecar racing, in which the Swallow 'Scrapper' was quite successful. Later, he had S.S.1 tourers prepared for the International Alpine Trial in 1933 and 1934, though the company's first notable competition success came when journalist Tommy Wisdom drove a works-prepared 2½-liter SS 100 to victory in the 1936 'Alpine' – much to the surprise of the Bugatti drivers!

It was the development of this car that gave Bill Heynes an aiming point when designing the XK engine – BWK 77's 3½-liter engine finally put out over 160bhp in racing trim. Yet Lyons' enthusiasm was tempered with caution: he had seen too many companies get so involved with motor racing that normal commercial considerations were ignored. Bankruptcy was often the ultimate result.

Thus it was that when Lyons finally produced a world-class competitive car – the XK 120 – he had to be persuaded

to allow it to be raced. Fortunately, the new car won first time out, in 1949 at the former bomber base at Silverstone. This encouraged him to enter (in the names of private owner-drivers) three XK 120s for the 1950 Le Mans 24-hour race. Leslie Johnson and Bert Hadley were gunning for second place against very specialized racing machinery when the clutch gave out, but the effort inspired Heynes to design a competition car using the main components of the XK 120 in a tubular frame.

A former aircraft engineer, Malcolm Sayer, was now working for Jaguar and designed the car's beautiful, all-enveloping aluminum body – the scuttle (cowl) section of which was affixed to the frame as Heynes discovered that this 'stressed skin' technique stiffened the whole structure very considerably. The engine and four speed gearbox were slightly modified XK 120 units, and the wishbone/torsion bar front suspension was also very similar to the production version. The rear axle, however, was sprung by a transverse torsion bar via trailing arms.

The XK 120C (for competition) was completed just in time

LEFT: With its beautiful Sayer-designed body, the C-type combined Jaguar looks with Le Mans winning performance. But the XK 120 was the first Jaguar at Le Mans – the car (RIGHT), driven by Haines and Clark, averaged almost 81mph to finish 12th in 1950.

LEFT: The C-type makes a fine road sportscar.

RIGHT: The D-type was highly scientific and appeared first in 'short nose' form.

BELOW: For 1955 the works cars were given a longer nose for aerodynamic reasons. The D-type was built with and without stabilizing tail fin.

for the 1951 Le Mans race, and although two of the three cars failed due to an identical fault (a fractured internal oil line), to the Jaguar team's intense relief Peter Whitehead and Peter Walker took the surviving car to an historic win. The first time a British car had won Le Mans since 1935, it boosted Jaguar's reputation and sales worldwide.

Le Mans always dominated Jaguar's thinking, and while the C-type was entered for other events, Lyons knew that nothing compared with the French 24-hour classic in terms of prestige. So it was a double disappointment when the 1952 race turned out to be a complete disaster . . .

Tales of the new Mercedes 300 SL coupe's enormous speed prompted a last-minute re-design of the C-type's bodywork, but the new drooping nose meant altering the cooling system. With no time for proper testing, it was only after practice laps just before the race that it was realized that the revised system wasn't working properly. All three cars ruined their engines and retired within the first hour of the race.

Le Mans 1953 was different. Jaguar appeared with a lighter, more powerful, Weber-carburetted C-type equipped with a 'secret weapon' – disk brakes. Inspired from aircraft practice, these had been developed by Jaguar and Dunlop and immediately proved their worth. The C-type drivers could brake hard and confidently lap after lap – the disks pulling the cars from well over 140mph on the

LEFT: Winning! The Ecurie Ecosse entered D-type on its way to victory, Le Mans 1957.

BELOW: The 'production' D-type at Laguna Seca vintage races, 1992.

RIGHT: Another D-type photographed head-on emphasizes the car's small frontal area.

BELOW RIGHT: The engine bay of an original 1954 D-type shows the car's alloy engine frame, later changed to steel.

Mulsanne straight to less than 30mph for the corner at the end – while the Ferrari and Alfa Romeo drivers had to conserve their drum brakes. Tony Rolt and Duncan Hamilton won with relative ease, becoming the first to win a Le Mans race at an average of over 100mph.

In all some 53 C-types were built; 43 being 'production' cars sold to customers who raced them all over the world, including America. But Jaguar were evolving a new car, the D-type. Undoubtedly the most advanced sports racing car of its time, it had a unique, aircraft-fuselage style aluminum centre 'tub,' with the engine carried – again aircraft fashion – on a lightweight tubular structure projecting from the front. The faithful XK engine now gave 250bhp and had dry sump lubrication (mainly to allow more oil to be carried, as Le Mans regulations prevented early replenishment). Disk brakes again featured (power operated by a pump driven from the new all-synchromesh gearbox), and the suspension was a development of the C-type's.

This compact design, clothed in a superb Sayer-designed body, was aerodynamically efficient for its day and presented a very small frontal area. The result was a car usually faster down the Mulsanne straight than the more powerful Ferraris and Maseratis. Three D-types entered the 1954 Le Mans race, and it was really through ill-luck that a Jaguar victory wasn't recorded – heavy rain negated much of their disk brakes' advantage, and over-efficient fuel filters delayed the cars through fuel starvation. Ferrari took the honours that year, by just two minutes.

The 1955 Le Mans was marred by the terrible accident involving a works Mercedes which took the lives of over 80 people. Mike Hawthorn and Ivor Bueb won in the new, 'long nose,' 275bhp D-type, the titanic battle between Hawthorn in the Jaguar and Juan Fangio in the new Mercedes 300 SLR ending when Mercedes withdrew. Enthusiasts argue to this day about who would have won if Fangio had continued.

Mercedes didn't enter at all in 1956, but the Jaguar team almost succeeded in wiping itself out when two D-types

RIGHT: The 1957 XK-SS evolved from the production D-type; note the full-width screen, bumpers and luggage rack. The passenger enjoyed under-floor heating courtesy of the exhaust!

LEFT: The engine was a full 250bhp D-type, providing 150mph-plus performance.

retired with accident damage on only the second lap. To make matters worse, the third car, driven by Hawthorn and Bueb, was badly delayed – a fuel line in the new Lucas fuel injection system had cracked. A D-type still won however; the private Ecurie Ecosse team's car running a consistent race to vanquish the Aston Martins.

The following year the D-type completely dominated Le Mans. Jaguar had officially retired from racing to concentrate on road car development, but continued to prepare cars for Ecurie Ecosse, Duncan Hamilton and other private entrants. Still superbly suited to the fast, smooth Le Mans circuit, D-types – the leading car now 3.8 liters – finished first, second, third, fourth and sixth!

Strangely, although D-types were entered at Le Mans up until 1960, not one was destined to even finish the event again. A change in regulations meant a maximum capacity of 3 liters, and the XK engine lost its legendary reliability. However, the car remains the most successful Le Mans Jaguar built.

Seventeen works D-types were made, and as with the C-type, Jaguar built a good number of 'production' examples – 45. Of these, 16 were made into XK-SS variants.

These fabulous, 150mph road cars were simply D-types fitted with a full width screen, minuscule bumpers, a luggage rack and other basic items of road equipment. It was hoped that they might be successful in SCCA sportscar racing, but although wins were recorded, the XK-SS was mostly regarded as a stupendously quick road car. Steve McQueen is said to have covered 80,000 miles in his!

Special mention should be made of Briggs Cunningham, America Cup winner and undoubtedly Jaguar's most active competitor in the US during the 1950s. In conjunction with Alfred Momo and Jaguar Cars Inc., the Cunningham team ran D-types extensively and won the Sebring 12-hour race in 1955.

The C- and D-type Jaguars were highly specialized cars, constructed purely to win Le Mans. This dictated the design priorities, and they scored on maximum speed and reliability rather than handling. Their relatively simple suspension systems were not suited to venues which, unlike Le Mans, were sinuous or poorly surfaced, and one reason Jaguar gave up motor racing was to concentrate on evolving a new suspension, which would reverse this situation in the next generation of sporting Jaguars.

CHAPTER 6
Consolidation

The years 1957 to 1960 represented a period of consolidation for Jaguar after a triumphant decade. No completely new models were released, but there were some very successful upgrades of established designs.

First, in May 1957, came the XK 150. A straightforward development of the XK 140, it used the same chassis except that at last disk brakes featured. The body was still identifiably 'XK', but featured a higher wingline and a wider, multi-slatted grille similar to the 3.4 sedan's. The interior was modernized with veneer finally disappearing from the Jaguar sportscar. Initially just fixed-head and drop-head styles were offered; the traditional roadster didn't arrive until March 1958.

This kept to a two-seat formula but progress had finally resulted in wind-up windows. As an antidote to the weight that the XK series was putting on, an 'S' engine option was now offered. This used the newly-developed 'straight port' cylinder head and three 2-inch rather than two 1¾-inch carburettors, moving the quoted horsepower of the 3442cc engine from 210 to 250. When, in October 1959, the 3781cc engine was offered, it could be had in normal 220bhp form, or in 265bhp 'S' guise. These options could be specified for all three body styles. The 3.8 XK 150S was a formidably quick machine, capable of over 135mph and 0-60mph in just 7.6 seconds – highly respectable even today!

The sedan range also received attention. In October 1958 the flagship Mk VIII was relaunched as the Mk IX; visually almost identical, the new model had the advantage of disk brakes and the new 3781cc engine. This pushed its top speed up from 105 to 115mph. Power steering was available, as was automatic or manual transmission.

THESE PAGES: The XK 150 gained weight but the fixed-head (LEFT) and drop-head (RIGHT) are both very rapid 'S' versions. The roadster cockpit (ABOVE) shows that veneer had left the Jaguar sportscar.

Then October 1959 saw the launch of the Mk 2. This exercise must rate as Jaguar's most successful facelift ever; using the 2.4/3.4 floorpan and internal structure, a completely new outer body transformed the car's appearance by greatly increasing the glass area. Gone were the previous chunky door and screen pillars, replaced by delicate chrome-plated frames.

Appearance and handling also benefitted from a wider rear axle, and the front suspension geometry was improved too. Inside the car, the seats, door panels and instrument panel were all modernized, while the 3.8-liter engine was added to the choice of 2.4 or 3.4-liter units. The 3.8 Mk 2 immediately became about the fastest four-seater car you could buy at any price, with the manual gearbox version capable of 0-60mph in just 8 seconds and a maximum speed of 125mph.

Only the 3.8-liter car was officially exported to the US, where it was even more popular than the previous Jaguar compact and for two years running was voted 'Best Imported Car.' Whereas 8460 LHD 3.4 sedans had been made, no less than 14,758 LHD 3.8 Mk 2s were completed. In all, 36,740 2.4/3.4 sedans were built, compared with 90,460 Mk 2s of all types. To this latter figure can be added 17,620 Daimler variants. This car ran with the Daimler 2.5-liter V8 engine which became available when Jaguar took over Britain's oldest motor manufacturer in 1960.

The 3.8 Mk 2 made a wonderful competition car, and it secured the first-ever European Touring Car Championship against Mercedes works opposition in 1963. It was also a consistent winner of the Tour de France Automobile. The Mk 2 certainly underpinned Jaguar's financial success and in 1959 Jaguar's profits exceeded £1m for the first time.

LEFT: A rarity. Sometimes an XK 150 would be ordered with pressed-steel wheels, which (as with previous XKs) came with spats.

ABOVE: The 113mph Mk IX sedan.

RIGHT: The brilliantly packaged Mk 2.

LEFT AND BELOW: The 3.8 Mk 2 combined high performance, luxury and style. Pressed steel or wire wheels could be fitted.

RIGHT: Stirling Moss flings a 3.8 around Silverstone in 1960 – but Roy Salvadori won the race in another Mk 2.

CHAPTER 7
New Cars for the Sixties

Sir William Lyons (he had been knighted in 1956) had a gift not only for styling cars, but for producing the right model at the right time. He ran no extensive market research operation, but seemed to have an instinctive knowledge of what his customers wanted.

Thus it was that the E-type, or XK-E as it was known in the US, was so completely correct for the 1960s. It was utterly modern; it was incredibly fast; and it was one of the most beautiful automobiles of all time. It matched perfectly the new decade of technical advances, optimism and growing disposable incomes.

The program to develop an XK sportscar replacement can be traced back to 1957 when a 2.4-liter dual-purpose road/race car prototype was made. Usually known as E1A, this car clearly bore the shape of the E-type to come, a shape honed from that of the D-type by aerodynamics expert Malcolm Sayer. The concept had been upgraded to 3.8 liters and a larger overall size by the time of the E-type's launch at the Geneva Salon in Switzerland in March 1961. The sheer beauty of the car was enough for many, but its looks were under-written by the extraordinary 150mph top speed recorded on road test. Yet, unlike a Ferrari or an Aston Martin, it was within the financial grasp of many people of the middle-income groups, priced at around $6000. Lyons had produced another miracle.

The E-type was a classic example of race-car technology being adapted for a road car, as it used many D-type princi-

ples – such as a monocoque centersection, an engine carried by a projecting framework, and a one-piece, un-stressed front which pivotted forward. But unlike the D-type, the new road car had independent rear suspension, a superbly effective system evolved by Bob Knight from a Talbot design of the 1920s, though Knight encapsulated it in a detachable rubber-mounted sub-frame and added inboard disk brakes. Combined with XK-type torsion bar/wishbone front suspension, the result was a sportscar which rode better than some sedans.

Produced in either roadster or fixed-head coupe form, the E-type went back to being a two-seater but was none the

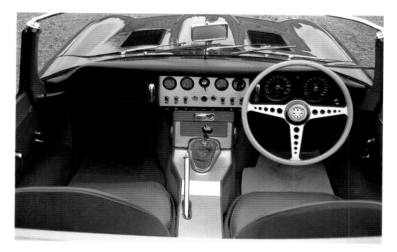

THESE PAGES: The 3.8 liter E-type in UK (LEFT) and US (RIGHT) specifications. The interior (ABOVE RIGHT) shows wood-rim wheel and aluminum dash of early examples.

worse for that. The ecstatic reception it received both at Geneva and a month later at New York mirrored that of the XK 120 some 14 years before – as did Lyons' total underestimation of demand. Just as with the XK 120 he had refused to believe that so many would want to buy the car, and had not allowed Bill Heynes to have the new sportscar properly tooled-up. But instead of the expected 20 cars a week, more like 120 were being ordered! Production was drastically up-graded but the labor-intensive build of the E-type remained, and for several years, Jaguar were unable to meet demand.

In another parallel with the XK 120, the E-type won its very first motor race – Graham Hill being victorious at Oulton Park. Briggs Cunningham ran a works-prepared fixed-head at Le Mans in 1962 finishing an excellent fourth, and from experience gained from this car and John Coombs' roadster (both of which were works prepared), a 'competition' E-type was built in 1963.

With a bodyshell and hard top in aluminum, the 'lightweight' E-type used an alloy-block, fuel-injected 3.8-liter engine which ultimately gave as much as 344bhp. The Cunningham team ran three at Le Mans in 1963 but a series of

THESE PAGES: The UK-spec. 3.8 roadster. The fixed-head was equally beautiful (ABOVE) – this car is missing its badge bar.

RIGHT: One of three competition E-types which Briggs Cunningham ran at Le Mans in 1963.

misfortunes resulted in a single ninth placing. German Jaguar distributor Peter Lindner perservered with his light-weight until 1964, but it failed at Le Mans that year and soon afterward Lindner was killed at Montlhery in the car.

Just 12 competition E-types were built (plus one steel-bodied coupe), but lacking full-time factory support and re-maining basically a road car design, its successes were spasmodic and only occasionally did it beat the lighter and much more specialized Ferrari GTO. Despite this fact, a number of top drivers raced the car, including Jackie Ste-wart and Graham Hill, while Bruce McLaren and Cunning-ham's lead driver Walt Hansgen drove in the 1964 Sebring 12 hours (though without great success). Jaguar's regular in-volvement with racing E-types ceased after 1964, though private owners continued, and on an amateur level the car remained competitive in such as SCCA racing for many years.

As we have seen, the E-type had been originally viewed by Lyons as a low-volume sideline, as Jaguar's main effort, and the major reason why the new independent rear sus-pension was developed, centred around the Mk IX replace-ment. Lyons had great hopes for the new Mk X, especially on the US market. It was the largest Jaguar so far: of unitary construction, with highly distinctive, rounded lines; and a radiator grille and front panel that projected forward at the top. The amount of room inside was enormous. It used the 3.8-liter triple carburetor E-type engine, mated to either a four-speed stick-shift or a Borg Warner automatic gearbox, and had a startling turn of speed for such a large car – 122mph and a 0-60mph time of 10.4 seconds. The new sus-pension provided remarkable handling qualities too, if the driver was not deterred by a fair degree of roll!

LEFT: The Mk X sedan (here in 4.2-liter form) offered spacious refinement.

RIGHT AND ABOVE RIGHT: E-types were often modified for racing – this car has three Weber carburetors in place of the standard triple 3Vs.

However, the Mk X proved to be one of the few cars where Lyons' judgment was not perfect. The all-important American market tended to view it as obese and lacking the grace of previous big Jaguars, while its reputation was blighted when early cars suffered from cooling system and electrical disorders. A disappointing sales record tells the story: compared with just over 47,200 Mk VII/VIII/IX sedans sold between 1951 and 1961, 13,382 Mk X 3.8s were pro-duced, or a little over 24,000 if one adds in the later 420G sold up until 1970.

Nevertheless, the Mk X was a remarkably refined and sophisticated car for its day, with ride qualities probably not exceeded by any other luxury sedan especially over poor surfaces. Its major engineering features had proved them-selves, and would be used to good effect in other, more successful Jaguars.

CHAPTER 8

Diversification and Multiplication

Jaguar always achieved much with the minimum of resources, thanks to Lyons' skill in extracting the maximum value from every engineering investment. So the plethora of new and revised models which sprung up during the middle and late sixties were all based on existing components and technology – mixed and stirred well.

The first variant combined a modified Mk 2 bodyshell with the Mk X's independent rear suspension. The result was the S-type sedan; it retained the Mk 2's door and roofline, but with an extended tail and a remodelled nose. Available with either 3.4 or 3.8-liter engines, it was more comfortable than the Mk 2 yet cheaper and more compact than the Mk X. The 3.8-liter version proved quite popular in the US, though it remains a rare car there compared with the Mk 2 itself.

As mentioned, the Mk 2 body was fitted with the Daimler V8 engine (plus a 'crinkly' radiator grille surround) and called the Daimler 2.5 V8; the only Daimler-engined Jaguar, it was produced from 1963 to 1969, and seemed to appeal to the older, less sporty driver. Performance was midway between the Jaguar 2.4 and 3.4 Mk 2.

Then in October 1964 came the most substantial revision of the trusty XK engine yet. The capacity was increased to 4.2 liters, the larger bores being accomodating by 'siames-

ing' them. Power output was said not to have altered, but torque was certainly increased. Along with the 4.2 engine came a new Jaguar-designed gearbox, as up-to-date as the previous one (with its prewar origins and non-synchromnesh first gear) had been outdated.

The E-type was given this new drive train along with a more powerful brake servo, new, wider seats; and many

LEFT: The S-type sedan with its remodeled front and rear.

RIGHT AND ABOVE RIGHT: The 4.2 E-type was externally almost identical to its 3.8-liter predecessor.

THESE PAGES: The 4.2-liter E-type retained covered headlamps and slim bumpers, while the engine still breathed through three SU carburetors.

detail improvements. Externally though, only the rear badging had changed, with the addition of '4.2' on the trunk lid; the diminutive bumpers and side lights remained. Similarly, the Mk X was upgraded with the larger engine and better gearbox.

March 1966 saw an important new development for the E-type – a two-plus-two version of the fixed-head, which extended both the car's wheelbase and its market, made its public debut at the New York Show. Jaguar's sportscar could once again be a family car, and the two-plus-two E-type soon sold as well as the normal fixed-head, especially as it alone offered automatic transmission.

In October of the same year, the melting pot was stirred again; in went the 4.2 engine, the S-type sedan body and the Mk X's front end, and out came the Jaguar 420 and (with crinkly grille) the Daimler Sovereign. Produced in fairly small numbers and rarely seen in the US, nevertheless the 420 and its Daimler cousin made further use of the Mk 2/S-type tooling, and kept up the flow of new products. At the same time, the 4.2 Mk X was upgraded to the 420G (for 'Grand') with a restyled interior, but its sales didn't show a similar uplift.

The final stage of getting the most from the Mk 2 tooling came in September 1967 when the 240 and 340 sedans were introduced. Their role was not only to provide an even cheaper entry level car, but (with typical Jaguar caution) also to act as a stand-by in case of problems with the production, or the popularity, of the brand new XJ6 scheduled for a 1968 launch.

These lightly modernized, slim-bumpered Mk 2s shed weight and costs. They also gained more power, thanks to their 2.4 or 3.4 engines being given the straight port 'gold top' cylinder head. Leather upholstery was now an extra, but on the other hand they were actually cheaper than the equivalant Mk 2s. A few 3.8 engined cars were built to special order, incidentally, but were never cataloged and never termed '380'; if anything they were 3.8 engined 340s.

Next, in October 1968, came a large-scale revision of the E-type. This was prompted mainly by looming safety and emission legislation in the States, but also by the experience gained over seven years of production. Although preceeded by what has colloquially come to be called the

LEFT: An early heavy-bumpered V8 Daimler-engined version of the Mk 2 alongside (foreground) the slim-bumpered 240 Jaguar.

RIGHT AND BELOW: The 240 auto interior – wood veneer remained but leather was an option – and grille detail.

BELOW LEFT: The Mk X became the more embellished 420G.

'Series 1½' car (basically a 4.2 E-type minus its headlamp covers), the Series 2 E-type was visually very different from its predecessor, having a larger 'mouth' for better cooling, open headlights set in big chrome bezels, larger sidelights front and rear, much improved brakes, and a 'safety' interior with recessed door and window handles. Mechanically, emission regulations had forced a change on US models from triple SU carburetors to two Strombergs, which reduced the car's top speed from nearly 150mph to around 137mph.

Meanwhile Sir William had been considering Jaguar's future. His only son, John, had been killed in an accident on the way to Le Mans in 1955 and there was no other obvious successor. So in 1966 from a position of strength – the company had achieved a record profit of £1,458,171 in 1965 – he negotiated a merger with the British Motor Corporation, owner of the Austin, Morris, MG, Riley and Wolseley marque names. It was sensible; Sir William foresaw that the situation for a small independent specialist company like Jaguar might become very difficult, and in particular he was concerned about the continuity of body supplies from Pressed Steel, now owned by BMC. The resulting parent company was called British Motor Holdings. Jaguar had, after 44 years, lost its total independence.

THESE PAGES: Ribbed camshaft covers arrived in the late-1960s for the XK engine (LEFT), while the Series 2 E-type (BELOW) gained larger sidelamps, a wider air intake, and (BOTTOM RIGHT) a modernized interior.

ABOVE RIGHT: Three superb Jaguars living in America – E-type, Mk 2 and XK 120.

CHAPTER 9
XJ6 and Acclamation

Ever since the early sixties work had been underway on a Mk X replacement. Much had been learned from the big Jaguar sedan, and it was apparent that the new car needed to be slightly shorter, narrower and lower. The aim was also that it should be quieter, faster and handle more nimbly. Yet costs must not mount so that the value-for-money factor would be lost.

That car was, of course, the XJ6, and it was to be Sir William Lyons' crowning glory. When it appeared in September 1968, it was clear that the new Jaguar displayed a formidable competence. It was quieter and rode better than a Rolls-Royce; it out-handled a Mercedes; it was faster than a Cadillac; and it looked more graceful than any of them. Bill Lyons had finally achieved the ambition he had expressed so clearly to Bill Heynes all those years ago. If there can be such a thing as the 'best' luxury car in the world, the XJ6 was surely a rightful claimant.

The car used the accumulated knowledge of automobile refinement that Bill Heynes and Bob Knight had acquired since the early 1950s. Yet the car's basic engineering was

not exotic, as it employed the same basic engine, transmission and suspension systems well-proven on the Mk X and other Jaguars. A 3-liter engine and a new multi-link rear suspension had been considered, but the production car remained faithful to the twin carburetor 4.2 engine (largely as used in the 420) and the excellent independent rear suspension first seen on the E-type. A 2.8-liter version of the XK 'six' was available in the UK and some European markets where there was a 3-liter tax break.

The XJ6 even when standing still appeared to grip the road, and by late 1960's standards its handling and road-holding were indeed awe-inspiring for what was still a large car – thanks in part to Dunlop producing a new, wide (205 section) low-profile radial tire especially for Jaguar. The interior was furnished with all the leather and walnut veneer you could wish for, and either an automatic gearbox or four-speed manual gearbox (with or without overdrive) could be specified.

After a slow start which created something of a black market (Jaguar were involved in prolonged negotiations

TOP LEFT: The XJ6 re-wrote the luxury car book; this is one of the first built.

LEFT AND RIGHT: The V12 engine and wider tires updated the E-type in 1971; power unit was fed by four 'emission' Stromberg carburetors.

over the bodyshell pricing!), XJ6 production built up rapidly. Exports to the all-important US mounted; 7384 Jaguars of all types reaching the US in the 12 months ending mid-September 1970 (compared with seven in 1947, 1552 in 1949/50, and 5716 in 1961/62 when the Mk 2 and E-type were nearing full production).

Yet the XJ6 was perceived by Jaguar as merely the first step. Right from the outset the intention was that it should have a multi-cylinder engine, but much as the XK 120 was used to give the new XK engine a low-volume trial run, so the new V12 engine arrived first in the E-type. This was re-launched in March 1971 as the Series 3. It was modernized with wider, XJ6-type tires covered by fender flares, a grille to the air intake, and a new interior. The roadster was now based on the two-plus-two floorpan, giving the occupants more room and an optional automatic gearbox (though the car still lacked rear seats).

The 5343cc all-aluminum V12 was soon hailed as perhaps the world's best production car engine. Jaguar's first V12 had grown from the XK unit and was a 5-liter racing-type, four-cam motor which turned out to be too bulky for production use (though it was used in the XJ13, Jaguar's still-born Le Mans car of 1966). The new 5.3-liter, 90 x 70mm engine was largely the brainchild of Walter Hassan, and featured flat cylinder heads with combustion chambers formed in the piston crowns. Even with four Stromberg carburetors it produced 270bhp, and gave the E-type back much of the performance it had lost over the years, despite the extra weight.

When this superbly smooth engine was combined with the innate refinement of the XJ sedan, the result was certainly a world-class, if thirsty (12mpg), automobile. The XJ12 was launched in August 1972, and was followed up in October by a longer wheelbase version.

The extra four inches were offered on the XJ6 too in Sep-

tember 1973, with the arrival of the Series 2 range of sedans. North American federal regulations influenced some of the changes – such as the raised bumpers – but there was also a modernized interior with stalk controls replacing some switches. A two-door coupe on the original wheelbase was also announced, available with six or 12 cylinder engines, though this most handsome of the XJ range did not enter production until April 1975 (even then, sales did not match up to Jaguar's expectations, perhaps because US purchasers reckoned to pay less for a two-door while Jaguar expected them to pay more!).

The last E-type was built in 1974; it was undeniably becoming old-fashioned, and forthcoming US safety regulations could not easily be met. Sales had slowed, and Jaguar issued the last 50 roadsters as special editions, each carrying an inscribed plaque signed by Sir William Lyons.

The E-type was never truly replaced, for the XJ-S of September 1975 was a suave grand tourer rather than an out-

ABOVE, LEFT AND ABOVE RIGHT: The Series 3 E-type roadster showing its flared wheel arches and radiator grille. The fixed-head (ABOVE RIGHT) and roadster shared the two-plus-two floorplan.

RIGHT: The XJ-S of 1975 was definitely 'GT,' not 'sports.'

THESE PAGES: The Series 3 sedan arrived for 1979, also in XJ12 form (BELOW). It achieved record sales in the US though not all were used everyday like the car shown at bottom right.

right sportscar. Undoubtedly the most refined high-performance coupe in the world, it used a short wheelbase version of the XJ floorpan and was powered by Jaguar's V12 engine (now with fuel injection). However, the new car's Sayer-originated styling proved controversial, for there was no open version available, and it was over twice the price of the V12 E-type. As a result, many enthusiasts both at home and abroad declined to buy it.

Nor was the situation within Jaguar much happier. Sir William had retired in March 1972 aged 70, very nearly 50 years after he had founded the business. F R W 'Lofty' England, former service director and racing team manager in the 1950s, succeeded him as chief executive but found little room for maneuver. BMH had merged with Leyland (truck builder and owner of the Triumph name) in May 1968, and the autonomy of Jaguar which Sir William thought had been assured within the British Leyland group did not materialize in practice.

Lofty England, having seen the company through a comparatively successful 1973, retired to leave the field free to the 34-year-old Geoffrey Robinson – who subsequently resigned in April 1975 when British Leyland tried to abolish Jaguar's board and amalgamate the company within a specialist car group. It was chiefly due to Bob Knight that Jaguar's heart, the engineering division, did retain its identity and independence.

Thus the Series 3 XJ range, when it arrived in March 1979, retained a 'real' Jaguar character. A crisper look had been achieved with a new roofline, and the interior was facelifted

too. There was an optional five-speed manual gearbox (rarely seen in the US); and the fuel injected 4.2-liter engine, first used in late-model Series 2 cars in the US market, was adopted as standard – along with the carbureted 3.4 unit which had first appeared in April 1975. The Series 3 was undoubtedly a better car than its predecessors, but muddled BL management and dropping morale within the company conspired to affect quality badly. There were quite severe problems; especially with the electrics (never a strong point on Jaguars) and the paintwork.

However, a ray of light came when Michael Edwardes was appointed to sort out the BL mess. He encouraged the

40-year-old John Egan (formerly of GM's AC Delco organization and who had later launched Unipart for British Leyland) to take the reinstated boss' job at Browns Lane. Joining in April 1980, Egan succeeded in gaining the confidence of the workforce, and made it his priority to build quality and reliability back into the product – the basic worth of which he was convinced of.

The results were dramatic; production soared and the US market took 15,059 Jaguars in 1983 compared with a disastrous 2943 in 1979. This export success, helped by a favorable £/$ relationship, was a vital factor in the company's return to profitability in the early 1980s. Much of this was built on an ever-improving Series 3 XJ6, but the XJ-S added its share when in July 1981 the HE version appeared. The V12 engine was given new 'high efficiency' cylinder heads developed by the Swiss engineer Michael May, but almost as important as a near 20mpg potential for the big GT was the replacement of its sombre interior by a new one brightened with wood veneer. From a near-terminal 1131 XJ-Ss made in 1980, 6000 were made in 1984. The car was performing on the track too – Tom Walkinshaw's racing XJ-S team won the Spa 24-hour race in Belgium, signaling a European motor sports revival for the marque.

The act of privatizing Jaguar followed. This was largely a political move by Mrs Thatcher's Conservative government, but flotation on the London and New York stock exchanges in August 1984 was an enormous success, and the offer was heavily over-subscribed. Once again, Jaguar was master of its own destiny, but for how long?

CHAPTER 10

XJ40 and Ford

The Series 3 XJ6, successful as it was, hadn't originally featured in the product plan at all – it was a brand new sedan, coded 'XJ40,' that should have appeared in the late 1970s. But the programme was late and, under the BL regime, beset with doubts, a third and final update of the existing XJ6 was carried out. This interim car proved so successful that more time could be spent developing the entirely new model, which finally emerged in October 1986, and had its North American launch at the New York show in April 1987.

It retained the XJ6 model name simply because that had garnered such international respect over the years. Producing a completely new car (there were virtually no carry-over

parts) was a stupendous effort by a tiny specialist company, and other manufacturers marveled that it was achieved at all – especially as it involved a new engine too. For although the twin-cam 3.6-liter AJ6 power unit had been offered in the XJ-S from 1983, its single-cam 2.9-liter sister had not.

The car's designer was Jim Randle, who had joined Jaguar from Rover in 1965. He had evolved a new, lighter, multi-link, 'compliant' rear suspension and refined the Series 3 front suspension. Trevor Crisp was largely reponsible for the new AJ6 family of engines, which gave the lighter XJ40s greater performance than the Series 3. But despite being the most tested Jaguar ever – there were now Jaguar bases in Phoenix, Arizona, and Timmins, Ontario, while the eight-mile Nardo circuit in Italy allowed flat-out motoring – it was a year before the new car achieved Series 3 standards of reliability.

XJ40 received its first upgrade in September 1989, the 3.6-liter engine growing to 3980cc, which increased power from the catalyst engine from 199bhp to 223bhp (manufacturer's horsepower figures now accorded more with the truth than in earlier decades!). Gone was the hi-tec fluorescent display instrument panel – it had been discovered that Jaguar owners preferred conventional dials set in veneer. In the US, the Vanden Plas Majestic XJ6 and the Collection Rouge XJ-S variants appeared, enhanced with special paint and trim.

Meanwhile the XJ-S hadn't been ignored. A low-volume cabriolet arrived with the 3.6-engined XJ-S in 1983, and

LEFT: The original XJ40 pictured with a Mk V11 in front of Glamis Castle in Scotland.

ABOVE: The 1990 model XJ6.

RIGHT: The Series 3 meanwhile lived on in XJ12/Daimler Double Six form until the end of 1992.

from 1985 it was available with the V12 engine too. The cabriolet was supplanted in March 1988 by a true convertible with power top (some while previously, Hess and Eisenhart in the US had converted the XJ-S with factory approval). The convertible V12 sold well in the US, especially in California.

October 1988 saw the surprise debut of the stunning XJ220 at the British Motor Show. This largely 'part-time' concept vehicle was built by Jim Randle and a few dedicated engineers at Jaguar's extensive new Whitley engineering facility, with much help from component firms. Such was its reception that this Keith Helfet-styled supercar was made a production reality by the new JaguarSport company, which had been formed 50/50 by Tom Walkinshaw's TWR group and Jaguar in May 1989.

In a remarkably rapid development and production programme, new XJ220s – now powered by a derivative of the TWR Jaguar twin-turbo 3.5-liter racing engine rather than the V12 of the prototype – were being driven from a new factory in Oxfordshire by mid-1992. The car did much to keep alive the glamour of the Jaguar name at a time when new products were few.

By the late 1980s, however, Sir John Egan (he had been knighted in 1986 for services to exports) and Jaguar were increasingly aware that in the face of massive competition from their traditional (and much larger) German rivals, and with a Japanese challenge in the luxury car market expected too, the company might not have the engineering or financial resources to fund the development of competitive

models in the future. Despite having just broken the 50,000 production barrier, profits were sliding as the $ lost value against the £. So when both GM and Ford made approaches, Jaguar listened.

It was, of course, Ford which won Jaguar's hand. Offered £6bn, Jaguar's shareholders voted by a 75 percent majority to accept the American company's bid, and in December 1989 Jaguar were again part of a large group. Why did Ford want Jaguar? It too was aware of the forthcoming crop of new luxury cars from Japan – Lexus, Infiniti and Acura – and considered that it would be better, and ultimately cheaper, to buy an established luxury brand name than to attempt to create a new one from scratch.

ABOVE LEFT AND LEFT: The 4.0-liter AJ6 engine was offered in the XJS convertible too, which also received an updated interior.

RIGHT AND ABOVE RIGHT: The 212mph XJ220 did much to raise Jaguar's high-performance profile in the early 1990s, with styling cues evocative of XJ13 and E-type features.

LEFT: The XJR 14 driven by
Warwick and Brundle at Monza,
May 1991.

BELOW: The Silk Cut sponsored
XJR 12 won at Le Mans in 1990.

RIGHT AND BELOW RIGHT: The
'Celebration Coupe' XJ-S was
created in 1988 to commemorate
Jaguar's first 'modern' Le Mans
win.

On the competitions front, the TWR Jaguar XJ-S team
had won the European Touring Car Championship in 1984,
while previously Bob Tullius's Virginia-based Group 44
team had moved from racing V12 E-types to winning the
Trans-Am championship with a space-framed XJ-S. Then
in 1982 they designed a new production-block V12 sports
racing car which three years later, in XJR-5 form, became
the first 'Jaguar' to race at Le Mans for 11 years (although the
two cars entered didn't finish).

In Europe the new TWR Jaguar team embarked on the
World Sportscar Championship in August 1985, and in 1986
ran their XJR-6 at Le Mans (though without a finish). However, in 1987 the Sportscar Championship fell to the team
which the following year recorded a historic Jaguar victory
at Le Mans with the V12-engined XJR9 LM – to the intense
delight of the 50,000-odd British fans there! The 1989 Le
Mans brought no win for Jaguar, but the marque was victorious in 1990, bringing Jaguar's Le Mans tally to seven.

TWR Inc now managed Jaguar's US racing effort and won
Daytona in January 1988. However, although TWR perservered over the next four years in the IMSA series and
recorded many fine individual victories, the 1992 season
closed still without Championship honours. But the January
1993 announcement of a racing XJ220 heralded Jaguar's
entry into GT racing that year.

Meanwhile Sir John Egan, as expected, departed, and,
after Ford veteran Bill Hayden drastically upgraded
Jaguar's manufacturing, in 1992 Nicholas Scheele took the
key post at Browns Lane. Quality was soon better than it

ever had been, and although Jaguar were terribly affected by the early-1990s depression (annual sales fell to 23,000 in 1992, less than the company had achieved in 1961), customer satisfaction rose.

No spectacular new models could be announced, but a systematic upgrading of the existing range took place. The 2.9-liter engine was replaced by a new, more powerful 3.2-liter unit when the 1991 models were announced in September 1990. All Jaguars now ran with a catalyst exhaust, and a Sports Handling Pack became a sedan option in most non-US markets (it had been standard on all six-cylinder XJ-S cars since 1987).

Then in May 1991, the XJS received a face-lift with what amounted to a new, higher-quality bodyshell made at Jaguar's new Venture Pressings factory at Telford. The same basic shape remained, but a new front and rear treatment modernized what had now become a classic design. Importantly, there was a new interior as well – gone at last were those strange barrel instruments! At the same time, the 4-liter AJ6 engine replaced the 3.6 as the alternative to the V12 engine in the coupe. The new model was the first six cylinder XJS offered in the US, going on sale from the autumn of 1991 (already 51 percent of XJ-Ss, or 4715 units in 1990, were being sent across the Atlantic).

The JaguarSport range continued, the 6-liter XJR-S first seen in August 1989 being revised in September 1991 with new body equipment and a 'tidied' engine bay, and the XJR 4-liter sedan was given a restyled body kit for the 1991 model year. The 4-liter XJS coupe and convertible became

available in the US, with the Getrag five-speed manual gearbox optional from the fall of 1992 – the first time a stick-shift Jaguar had been marketed in the US since the Series 3 E-type!

The UK Motor Show in October 1992 saw the first fruits of Jaguar's new Special Vehicle Operations, which had sprung from the skilled band of men who had assembled the coachbuilt Daimler DS 420 Limousine since 1968. This stately machine, which used an extended Mk X floorpan, ceased production in the fall of 1992, and the new long wheelbase XJ6 which appeared at the Show was, if not an

LEFT: The 6-liter XJR-S and a 'Jaguar' fighter aircraft.

BELOW: Specifications of the new 155mph XJ12 and Daimler Double-Six announced in February 1993 included a new four-speed auto transmission.

exact replacement, very much welcomed by the carriage trade. Also displayed for the first time were the Insignia models; these being finished to the customer's individual choice from a new range of special paints and trims. •

A major product announcement of 1993 was the new V12-engined sedan, which made its entrance at the Amsterdam Show in February. This car, with a 6-liter power unit and a specification to match any Mercedes, was a direct replacement for the Series 3 XJ12 which had soldiered on, at the rate of 300 or 400 units a year, after the Series 3 XJ6 was discontinued at the end of 1986. The XJ12 had built up a small but dedicated following as a 'living classic,' especially in Japan, and it was not until 30 November 1992 that the

final Series 3 XJ12 – actually a Daimler Double Six – drove from Track Six at Browns Lane. It was the last of some 177,240 original-type XJ6/XJ12 cars made since 1968.

Although the early years of the 1990s were clouded by economic depression in the UK, much of Europe, the US, and even – finally – Japan, it appeared certain that the luxury car market would blossom again. Ford had displayed an understanding of the uniqueness and individuality of Jaguar, while at the same time used their expertise to massively upgrade the quality of the product. The result: better, more reliable Jaguars which retain their true character – a character established by a young Blackpool man over 70 years ago.

Index

Page numbers in *italics* refer to illustrations

ACKNOWLEDGMENTS

The author and publisher would like to thank David Eldred the designer, Stephen Small the editor and picture researcher, Veronica Price and Nicki Giles for production, and Ron Watson for providing the index. The following individuals and agencies provided photographic material:

Bison Books, pages: 34(top), 70(bottom).
Neill Bruce, pages: 7, 10, 15, 16, 18, 19(bottom), 22(bottom), 23(top), 32(bottom), 36, 37, 38(bottom), 39, 42, 46, 48, 52, 54(top), 56(top), 57(bottom), 61(bottom).
Neill Bruce/Nigel Dawes Collection, pages: 14(bottom), 24, 27, 30, 33, 44, 47(bottom), 49(both), 51(both), 53.
Neill Bruce/Midland Motor

Museum, pages: 1, 12, 20, 21(bottom), 23(bottom), 47(top), 50, 69(both).
Neill Bruce/The Peter Roberts Collection, pages: 19(top), 43(top).
David Hodges, page: 68(top).
Andrew Morland, page: 56(bottom).
Don Morley, pages: 25, 26(both).
National Motor Museum, Beaulieu, pages: 22(top),

35(bottom), 40, 41,(top/Nicky Wright), 58(bottom), 59, 62(top), 62(bottom/Nicky Wright), 65(bottom).
Paul Skilleter, pages: 2-3, 4-5, 6, 8(both), 9, 11, 13(both), 14(top), 17(both), 21(top), 28, 29(all three), 31, 32(top), 34(bottom), 35(top), 38(top), 41(bottom), 43, 45(both), 54(bottom), 57(top), 58(top), 60(both), 61(top), 63(both), 64, 65(top), 66(both), 67(both), 68(bottom), 70(top).